Alfred Perceval Graves

Father O'Flynn

And Other Irish Lyrics

Alfred Perceval Graves

Father O'Flynn
And Other Irish Lyrics

ISBN/EAN: 9783744726733

Printed in Europe, USA, Canada, Australia, Japan

Cover: Foto ©Thomas Meinert / pixelio.de

More available books at **www.hansebooks.com**

FATHER O'FLYNN,

And other Irish Lyrics.

BY

ALFRED PERCEVAL GRAVES.

LONDON:
SWAN SONNENSCHEIN & CO.,
PATERNOSTER SQUARE.
1889.

TO

MARY M. F. SEYMOUR,

THIS BOOK OF IRISH LYRICS

IS AFFECTIONATELY DEDICATED.

PREFACE.

BUT a very few words are called for from me by way of preface. This book is a selection from my three volumes of Irish Lyrics, *Songs of Killarney*, *Irish Songs and Ballads*, and *Songs of Old Ireland* (fifty Irish Songs and Ballads arranged to old Irish Airs by Dr. Charles Villiers Stanford). The two earlier volumes are out of print, after running through several editions, and I am advised that there is an increasing demand for Irish Poetry, which justifies my venturing upon a reprint of those of my Lyrics which have found most favour in the Old and New Worlds.

I have been very kindly assisted in the selection by my father, the Bishop of Limerick, my uncle, the

Rev. Robert Perceval Graves, my cousin, Mr. Rolleston, and my friend Professor Dowden.

Space does not permit of my giving notes explanatory of my obligations to Celtic and early Anglo-Irish Ballad-writers in this little book. But I have been at the utmost pains to do so in my second and third volumes, which may be consulted by the curious.

CONTENTS.

	PAGE
FATHER O'FLYNN	9
THE IRISH SPINNING WHEEL	11
THE ROSE OF KENMARE	15
RIDING DOUBLE	19
RIDING TREBLE	20
BAT OF THE BRIDGE	22
FAN FITZGERL	27
THE LIGHT IN THE SNOW	29
NANCY, THE PRIDE OF THE WEST	32
THE WRECK OF THE AIDEEN	34
KITTY BAWN	36
SAVING THE TURF	37
LOOBEEN	38
THE BLACK '46	40
THE HOUR WE PARTED	43
THE IRISH EXILE'S LOVE	45
THE FOGGY DEW	46
FIXIN' THE DAY	48
MOLLEEN OGE	51
IRISH LULLABY	53
THE MILL SONG	54
THE LITTLE RED LARK	56
LOVE'S WISHES	57
A LAMENTATION	58
THE BANKS OF THE DAISIES	59
THE ROSE-TREE IN FULL BEARING	60
HERRING IS KING	62

CONTENTS.

	PAGE
MY LOVE'S AN ARBUTUS	64
THE BLUE, BLUE SMOKE	66
'TWAS PRETTY TO BE IN BALLINDERRY	69
OH THOU OF THE BEAUTIFUL HAIR	70
MOLLY HEWSON	71
THE CONFESSION	72
WITH THE NORTH	74
THE POTATO BLOSSOM	77
MAUREEN, MAUREEN	84
ONE SUNDAY AFTER MASS	85
WHEN I ROSE IN THE MORNING	87
THE GIRL I LEFT BEHIND ME	88
THE SAILOR GIRL	90
JACK THE JOLLY PLOUGHBOY	91
A LOVE SONG	92
SPINNING-WHEEL SONG	94
THE LIMERICK LASSES	95
O'FARRELL THE FIDDLER	99
LONESOME LOVERS	104
THE WHITE BLOSSOM'S OFF THE BOG	109
JENNY, I'M NOT JESTING	111
ANCIENT LULLABY	113
THE FOX HUNT	115
COLLEEN OGE ASTHORE	117
I ONCE LOVED A BOY	120
THE SONG OF THE FAIRY KING	121
WHEN SHE ANSWERED ME	123
WITH FLUTTERING JOY	124
THE HOUR I PROVE FALSE	125
'TIS A PITY I CAN'T SEE MY LOVE	126
SONG	127
GOOD NIGHT	128

FATHER O'FLYNN.

OF priests we can offer a charmin' variety,
Far renowned for larnin' and piety;
Still, I'd advance ye, widout impropriety,
    Father O'Flynn as the flower of them all.

CHORUS.—*Here's a health to you, Father O'Flynn,*
    Slainté,* and slainté, and slainté agin;
    Powerfulest preacher, and
    Tinderest teacher, and
    Kindliest creature in ould Donegal.

Don't talk of your Provost and Fellows of Trinity,
Famous for ever at Greek and Latinity,
Dad and the divels and all at Divinity,
    Father O'Flynn 'd make hares of them all!
    Come, I vinture to give ye my word,
    Never the likes of his logic was heard,

---

* Your health.

Down from mythology
Into thayology,
Troth ! and conchology if he'd the call.

CHORUS.—*Here's a health to you, Father O'Flynn,*
Slainté, and slainté, and slainté agin ;
Powerfulest preacher and
Tinderest teacher, and
Kindliest creature in ould Donegal.

Och ! Father O'Flynn, you've the wonderful way wid you,
All ould sinners are wishful to pray wid you,
All the young childer are wild for to play wid you,
You've such a way wid you, Father avick ! *
Still, for all you've so gentle a soul,
Gad, you've your flock in the grandest control ;
Checking the crazy ones,
Coaxin' onaisy ones,
Liftin' the lazy ones on wid the stick.

CHORUS.—*Here's a health to you, Father O'Flynn,*
Slainté, and slainté, and slainté agin ;
Powerfulest preacher, and
Tinderest teacher, and
Kindliest creature in ould Donegal.

---

* " My son," an obvious Irish bull.

And though quite avoidin' all foolish frivolity,
Still at all seasons of innocent jollity,
Where was the play-boy could claim an equality
  At comicality, Father, wid you?
    Once the Bishop looked grave at your jest,
    Till this remark set him off wid the rest:
      "Is it lave gaiety
      All to the laity?
    Cannot the clargy be Irishmen too?

CHORUS.—*Here's a health to you, Father O'Flynn,*
  Slainté, and slainté, and slainté agin;
    Powerfulest preacher, and
    Tinderest teacher, and
  Kindliest creature in ould Donegal.

THE IRISH SPINNING WHEEL.

"SING me a song,
  Shiel, Shiel—
As my foot on the reel
Goes guidin' the wheel
  Along.

For I keep better time
To a musical rhyme,
Than without."

"No doubt—
But Roseen, yourself start a tune—
For I've heard
How a bird
That sings by the light of the moon,
Away over the ocean,
Once took up a notion,
The vain little elf, that he'd fly
To Ireland itself on the sly,
And prove all the songs of our sky
Wid the tone
Of his own
Could never at all at all vie;
And he thought himself surely the best,
And 'twas true for him, p'r'aps, of the rest;
But we've all understood
Meetin' you in the wood,
As you warbled 'The Land of the West,'
He should say,
He'd no chance
Wid you;

So away
    Into France
      He flew."

"Behave, Shiel,
  Yerra, don't you feel
  How your blarneyin' talk is delayin' my reel ;
    If you won't sing a song,
    As I'm spinnin' along,
  Be off—for you're idlin' myself and the wheel."

"Is it so?
  O! Vo!
  If off I should go
    Widout that I make you the music, machree,
      Down here,
      My dear,
      From this seat
      At your feet
    I'll up wid the song that's the dearest to me."

SONG.

  Show me a sight,
    Bates for delight
An ould Irish wheel wid a young Irish girl at it.

O! No!
Nothin' you'll show
Aquals her sittin' an' takin' a twirl at it.

Look at her there,
Night in her hair—
The blue ray of day from her eye laughin' out on us!
Faix an' a foot,
Perfect of cut,
Peepin' to put an end to all doubt in us

That there's a sight,
Bates for delight
An ould Irish wheel wid a young Irish girl at it.
O! No!
Nothin' you'll show
Aquals her sittin' an' takin' a twirl at it.

See! the lamb's wool
Turns coarse an' dull
By them soft, beautiful, weeshy,* white hands of her.
Down goes her heel,
Roun' runs the wheel,
Purrin' wid pleasure to take the commands of her;
For show me a sight, etc.

---

* Little.

Talk of Three Fates,
Seated on seats,
Spinnin' and shearin' away till they've done for me:
You may want three
For your massacree,
But one fate for me, boys, and only the one for me.

And
Isn't that fate
Pictured complate,
An ould Irish wheel wid a young Irish girl at it?
O! No!
Nothin' you'll show
Aquals her sittin' an' takin' a twirl at it.

THE ROSE OF KENMARE.

I've been soft in a small way
On the girleens of Galway,
And the Limerick lasses have made me feel quare;
But there's no use denyin'
No girl I've set eye on
Could compate wid Rose Ryan of the town of Kenmare.

O, where
Can her like be found?
Nowhere,
The country round,
Spins at her wheel
   Daughter as true,
Sets in the reel,
   Wid a slide of the shoe
     a slinderer,
     tinderer,
     purtier,
     wittier colleen than you,
Rose, aroo!

Her hair mocks the sunshine,
And the soft, silver moonshine
Neck and arm of the colleen complately eclipse;
Whilst the nose of the jewel
Slants straight as Carn Tual
From the heaven in her eye to her heather-sweet lips.

O, where, etc.

Did your eyes ever follow
The wings of the swallow
Here and there, light as air, o'er the meadow field glance?

For if not you've no notion
Of the exquisite motion
Of her sweet little feet as they dart in the dance.

    O, where, etc.

If y'inquire why the nightingale
Still shuns the invitin' gale
That wafts every song-bird but her to the West,
Faix she knows, I suppose,
Ould Kenmare has a Rose
That would sing any Bulbul to sleep in her nest.

    O, where, etc.

When her voice gives the warnin'
For the milkin' in the mornin'
Ev'n the cow known for hornin' comes runnin' to her pail;
The lambs play about her
And the small bonneens * snout her,
Whilst their parints salute her wid a twisht of the tail.

    O, where, etc.

When at noon from our labour
We draw neighbour wid neighbour
From the heat of the sun to the shilter of the tree,

---

* Young pigs.

Wid spuds * fresh from the bilin'
And new milk you come smilin',
All the boys' hearts beguilin', alannah machree! †

  O, where, etc.

But there's one sweeter hour
When the hot day is o'er
And we rest at the door wid the bright moon above,
And she sittin' in the middle,
When she's guessed Larry's riddle,
Cries, "Now for your fiddle, Shiel Dhuv, Shiel Dhuv."

  O, where
 Can her like be found?
  Nowhere,
 The country round,
 Spins at her wheel
  Daughter as true,
 Sets in the reel,
  Wid a slide of the shoe,
   a slinderer,
   tinderer,
   purtier,
  wittier colleen than you,
 Rose, aroo!

---

* Potatoes.   † My heart's delight.

RIDING DOUBLE.

Trottin' to the fair,
   Me and Moll Malony,
Sated, I declare,
   On a single pony;
How am I to know that
   Molly's safe behind,
Wid our heads in oh! that
   Awk'ard way inclined?
By her gintle breathin'
   Whispered past my ear,
And her white arms wreathin'
   Warm around me *here*.
Trottin' to the fair,
   Me and Moll Malony,
Sated, I declare,
   On a single pony.

Yerrig! * Masther Jack,
   Lift your fore-legs higher,
Or a rousin' crack
   Surely you'll require.

---

* Gee up!

"Ah!" says Moll, "I'm frightened
 That the pony 'll start,"
And her hands she tightened
 On my happy heart;
Till, widout reflectin'
 'Twasn't quite the vogue,
 Somehow, I'm suspectin'
 That I snatched a pogue.*
Trottin' to the fair,
 Me and Moll Malony,
Sated, I declare,
 On a single pony.

RIDING TREBLE.

Joultin' to the fair,
 Three upon the pony,
That so lately were
 Me and Moll Malony.
"How can three be on, boy?
 Sure, the wife and you,
Though you should be *wan*, boy,
 Can't be more nor *two*."

---

* A kiss.

Arrah, now then may be
   You've got eyes to see
That this purty baby
   Adds us up to *three*.
Joultin' to the fair,
   Three upon the pony,
That so lately were
   Me and Moll Malony.

Come, give over, Jack,
   Cap'rin' and curvettin',
All that's on your back
   Foolishly forgettin';
For I've tuk the notion
   Wan may cant'rin' go,
Trottin' is a motion
   I'd extind to *two*;
But to travel steady
   Matches best with *three*,
And we're that already,
   Mistress Moll and me.
Joultin' to the fair,
   Three upon the pony,
That so lately were
   Me and Moll Malony.

BAT OF THE BRIDGE.

On the bridge of Dereen,
    Away up by Killarney,
You'll be sure to be seein'
    Poor Batsy O'Kearney
A big stick in the air
    So lazily swingin',
Smokin' and jokin'
    And carelessly singin'
Some snatch of a song,
    Out over the river,
As it rushes along·
    For iver and iver
To the Bay of Kenmare.

    Six foot six
    Is the fix
    Of his height,
    Honour bright!
Forty-eight the diminsion
    Round his ribs by my inchin;
It's murther to say
    Such a man's thrun away.

He's the last to delay
    And the earliest comer
On the bridge by the bay,
    Winter and summer.
Do you question why so?
    What keeps him for iver
Smokin' and jokin'
    And out on the river
That rushes below,
    Serenadin' so gaily?
'Twas the cowardly blow
    Of a tinker's shillelagh
Left the proper man so.

But you're wonderin', why,
    How at all it could happen
Such a broth of a boy
    Got the scandalous rappin'.
'Twas September fair day,
    And the Adragole faction
Wid Dereen for the green
    And the bridge were in action;
And from off the bridge road,
    Wid his cudgel so clever,

Bat was leatherin' a load
   Of Cork men for ever,
Just as if it was play.

When up from beneath,
   Still further and further,
Houldin' tight in his teeth
   A stick that was murther,
That black tinker stole,
   By the ivy boughs clingin',
On the edge of the bridge
   The knees softly swingin';
And, unknownst at his back,
   From the wall of the river
Fetched O'Kearney a crack,
   That left him for iver
Wid a poor, puzzled poll.

Did he fall? Not at all!
   But he picked off that tinker
Like a snail from the wall
   And before you could think or
Repate your own name,
   Cot the stick from the ruffi'n,

Knocked him dead on the head,
    And widout shroud or coffin
Tossed him into the tide.
And his black corpse for ever
    From Ireland should glide,
For her good soil could never
    Cover up such a shame.

Thin backward agin
    Wid a bitter screech flyin'
On the Adragole men,
    Just as they were cryin',
"The bridge is our own"—
    In their thick, like a flail, he
Swung, till it sung,
    The tinker's shillelagh;
So that staggerin' down,
    Broken and batthered,
Out of the town
    All Adragole scatthered
Before Batsy alone.

Ever since which
    Poor Bat's only iday
Is to sit on the bridge,
    Wet day or dry day,

Wid that stick in his fist;
   And no tinkerin' fellas
Dare to come there
   Wid their pots and their bellas,*
And all Adragole
   Takes the ford down the river,
For fear that the fool
   On the bridge-end for iver
Should give them a twist.

So he's come by a name,
   The English of which, sir,
Translatin' that same,
   Is "Bat of the Bridge," sir.
But the hour's growin' late;
   Good-night and safe journey!
It's afloat in your boat
   You should be, Doctor Corney.
By myself, now, bad scran
   To the tribe of the tinkers,
For they've left a good man,
   Like a horse widout blinkers,
All bothered and bate.

---

* Bellows.

Six foot six
Is the height
Of poor Batsy to-night,
Forty-eight the diminsion
Round his ribs by my inchin',
It's murthur, I say,
Such a man's thrun away.

FAN FITZGERL.

Wirra, wirra ollogone ! *
Can't ye lave a lad alone,
Till he's proved there's no tradition left of any other girl—
Not even Trojan Helen,
In beauty all excellin',—
Who's been up to half the divelment of Fan Fitzgerl?

Wid her brows of silky black
Arched above for the attack,
Her eyes they dart such azure death on poor admirin' man;
Masther Cupid, point your arrows,
From this out, agin the sparrows,
For your bested at Love's archery by young Miss Fan.

* Expressions of grief.

See what showers of goolden thread
Lift and fall upon her head,
The likes of such a trammel-net at say was niver spread;
For whin accurately reckoned,
'Twas computed that each second
Of her curls has cot a Kerryman and kilt him dead.

Now mintion, if ye will,
Brandon Mount and Hungry Hill,
Or Ma'g'llicuddy's Reeks renowned for cripplin' all they can;
Still the country side confisses
None of all its precipices
Cause a quarther of the carnage of the nose of Fan.

But your shatthered hearts suppose
Safely steered apast her nose,
She's a current and a reef beyant to wreck them rovin' ships.
My maning it is simple,
For that current is her dimple,
And the cruel reef 'twill coax ye to 's her coral lips.

I might inform ye further
Of her bosom's snowy murther,
And an ankle ambuscadin' through her gown's delightful whirl;

> But what need, when all the village
> Has forsook its peaceful tillage
And flown to war and pillage—all for Fan Fitzgerl !

THE LIGHT IN THE SNOW.

Oh, Pat, the bitter day when you bravely parted from us,
　The mother and myself on the cruel quays of Cork :
When you took the long kiss, and you gave the faithful
　　promise
　That you'd soon bring us over to be wid you at New
　　York.

But the times they grew worse through the wild, weary
　　winter,
　And my needle all we had to find livin' for us two ;
While the mother drooped and drooped till I knelt down
　　forenint her
　And closed her dyin' eyes, dear,—but still no word of
　　you.

Then the neighbours thought you false to me, but I knew
    you better,
  Though the bud became the leaf, and the corn began to
    start ;
And the swallow she flew back, and still sorra letter ;
  But I sewed on and on, Pat, and kep' a stout heart.

Till the leaves they decayed, and the rook and the starlin'
  Returned to the stubble ; and I'd put by enough
To start at long last in search of my darlin',
  Alone across the ocean so unruly and rough.

Until at the end, very weak and very weary,
  I reached the overside, and started on my search ;
But no account for ever of Patrick for his Mary,
  By advertisin' for you, dear, or callin' you in church.

Yet still I struggled on, though my heart was almost broken
  And my feet torn entirely on the rough, rugged stone ;
Till that day it came round, signs by and by token,
  The day five year that we parted you, mavrone.

Oh ! the snow it was sweepin' through the dark, silent city,
  And the cruel wind it cut through my thin, tattered gown;

Still I prayed the good God on His daughter to take pity;
    When a sudden, strange light shone forenint me up the town.

And the light it led on till at last right opposite
    A large, lonely house it vanished as I stood;
Wid my heart axing wildly of me, was it, oh, was it
    A warnin' of ill or a token of good?

Then the light kindled up agin, brighter and bigger,
    And I saw my own shadow across the window cast,
While close, close, and closer to it stole a man's figure,
    And I fainted, as you caught me in your true arms at last.

Then Pat, my own Pat, I saw that you were altered
    To the shadow of yourself by the fever on the brain!
While "Mary, Mary darlin'," at last your lips they faltered,
    "You've given your poor Patrick his mem'ry back again."

And the good, gentle priest, when he comes, is never weary
    Of sayin', as he spakes of that light in the snow,
"The Lord heard your prayer, and in pity for you, Mary,
    Restored Pat the raison that he lost long ago."

NANCY, THE PRIDE OF THE WEST.

We have dark lovely looks on the shores where the Spanish
   From their gay ships came gallantly forth,
And the sweet shrinking violets sooner will vanish
   Than modest blue eyes from our north;
But oh! if the fairest of fair-daughtered Erin
   Gathered round at her golden request,
There's not one of them all that she'd think worth comparing
   With Nancy, the pride of the west.

You'd suspect her the statue the Greek fell in love with,
   If you chanced on her musing alone,
Or some goddess great Jove was offended above with,
   And chilled to a sculpture of stone;
But you'd think her no colourless, classical statue,
   When she turned from her pensive repose,
With her glowing grey eyes glancing timidly at you,
   And the blush of a beautiful rose.

Have you heard Nancy sigh? then you've caught the sad echo
   From the wind harp enchantingly borne.
Have you heard the girl laugh? then you've heard the first cuckoo
   Carol summer's delightful return;

And the songs that poor, ignorant, country folk fancy
    The lark's liquid raptures on high,
Are just old Irish airs from the sweet lips of Nancy,
    Flowing up and refreshing the sky.

And though her foot dances so soft from the heather
    To the dew-twinkling tussocks of grass,
It but warns the bright drops to slip closer together
    To image the exquisite lass;
We've no men left among us, so lost to emotion,
    Or scornful, or cold to her sex,
Who'd resist her, if Nancy once took up the notion
    To set that soft foot on their necks.
Yet, for all that the bee flies for honey-dew fragrant
    To the half-opened flower of her lips,
And the butterfly pauses, the purple-eyed vagrant,
    To play with her pink finger-tips;
From all human lovers she locks up the treasure
    A thousand are starving to taste,
And the fairies alone know the magical measure
    Of the ravishing round of her waist.

THE WRECK OF THE AIDEEN.

Is it cure me, docthor darlin'? an ould boy of siventy-four,
Afther soakin' off Berehaven three and thirty hour and more,
Wid no other navigation underneath me but an oar.

God incrase ye, but it's only half myself is livin' still,
An' there's mountin' slow but surely to my heart the dyin' chill;
God incrase ye for your goodness, but I'm past all mortial skill.

But ye'll surely let them lift me, won't you, docthor, from below?
Ye'll let them lift me surely—very soft and very slow—
To see my ould ship, Aideen, wanst agin before I go?

Lay my head upon your shoulder; thank ye kindly, docthor dear.
Take me now; God bless ye, Cap'n! now together! sorra fear!
Have no dread that ye'll distress me—now, agin, ochone!
   I see her.

Ologone! my Aideen's Aideen, christened by her laughin' lips,
Wid a sprinkle from her finger as ye started from the slips,
Thirty year ago come Shrovetide, like a swan among the ships.

And we both were constant to ye till the bitter, bitter day,
Whin the typhus took my darlin', and she pined and pined away,
Till yourself's the only sweetheart that was left me on the say.

So through fair and foul we'd travel, you and I thin,— usen't we?
The same ould coorse from Galway Bay, by Limerick and Tralee,
Till this storm it shook me overboard, and murthered you, machree.

But now, agra, the unruly wind has flown into the west,
And the silver moon is shinin' soft upon the ocean's breast,
Like Aideen's smilin' spirit come to call us to our rest.

Still the sight is growin' darker, and I cannot rightly hear;
The say's too cold for one so old; O, save me, Cap'n, dear!
Now it's growin' bright and warm agin, and Aideen, Aideen's here.

KITTY BAWN.

BEFORE the first ray of blushing day,
   Who should come by but Kitty Bawn?
With her cheek like the rose on a bed of snows,
   And her bosom beneath like the sailing swan.
   I looked and looked till my heart was gone.

With the foot of the fawn she crossed the lawn,
   Half confiding and half in fear;
And her eyes of blue they thrilled me through,
   One blessèd minute; then like the deer,
   Away she darted, and left me here.

Oh! Sun, you are late at your golden gate,
   For you've nothing to show beneath the sky
To compare to the lass who crossed the grass
   Of the shamrock field ere the dew was dry,
   And the glance that she gave me as she went by.

SAVING THE TURF.

CUTTIN' the turf, cuttin' the turf, with our feet on the shinin' slawn ! *
Cuttin' the turf, cuttin' the turf, till the cows come home to the bawn !
Footin' † the turf, footin' the turf, footin' and turnin' our best,
Footin' the turf, turnin' the turf, till the rook flies home to her nest !
Settin' ‡ the turf, settin' the turf, hither and over the land,
Settin' the turf, settin' the turf, till the say-turn § sinks on the strand !
Drawin' the turf, drawin' the turf, with our ponies and asses away,
Drawin' the turf, drawin' the turf, till the boats are out in the bay !
Rickin' the turf, rickin' the turf, safe in the haggard ‖ at last,
To keep and to comfort us all from the rage of the rain and the blast.

---

* The narrow Irish spade.   † Laying out the sods lengthwise.
‡ Setting the sods up endways.   § The breeze from the sea.
‖ Hay-yard.

LOOBEEN.

Bridgid.

Ere the sun began to peep,
    Out I wandered through our orchard.

Rosy.

Since you couldn't quiet sleep
    By the thoughts of Torlogh tortured;
For 'tis rumoured how of late,
    By his manly beauty melted,
With your pippin, plump and straight
    At the boy in vain you pelted.*

Bridgid.

Yes: Saint Bridgid, for my sake
    Interferin' with that apple,
Rolled it on to Rory Blake,
    And we're goin' to the chapel.

Rosy.

So you've handsome Rory fast!
    Girls, go set the secret spreadin',

---

* A rural practice that at once suggests Virgil's "malo me Galate petit."

That when solemn Lent is past
   We shall dance at Bridgid's weddin'!
Now, since all her news is out,
   Nora, see can you discover,
Eastward, westward, north, or sout',
   Where's the boy I'd make my lover?

NORA.

Murt na Mo you wish to wed?

ROSY.

Now that notion just be sparin'!
With a hornet at my head
   I'd as soon hop over Erin.
Come, I'll give a handsome hint,
   Girls, should set you rightly guessin'.
How is this? To school I wint,
   Till my master learnt my lesson.

NORA.

At the night-school—I've the whole,—
   With her make-believe-be-learnin',
'Tis the model-teacher's * poll
   That complately she's been turnin'.

---

* Teacher of a Government Model School.

Rosy.

Yes! I've clever Phelim fast.

Nora.

Girls, go set the secret spreadin',
That when solemn Lent is past
  We shall dance at Rosy's weddin'.

THE BLACK '46.

A RETROSPECT.

Out away across the river,
  Where the purple mountains meet,
There's as green a wood as iver
  Fenced you from the flamin' heat;
And oppósite, up the mountain,
  Seven ancient cells ye'll see,
And, below, a holy fountain
  Sheltered by a sacred tree;
While between, across the tillage,
  Two boreens * full up wid broom
Draw ye down into a village '
  All in ruin on the coom,†

---

* Narrow lanes.   † Valley.

For the most heart-breakin' story
  Of the fearful famine year
On the silent wreck before ye
  You may read charáctered clear.
You are young, too young for ever
  To rec'llect the bitter blight,
How it crept across the River
  Unbeknownst beneath the night;
Till we woke up in the mornin',
  And beheld our country's curse
Wave abroad its heavy warnin',
  Like the white plumes of a hearse.

To our gardens, heavy-hearted,
  In that dreadful summer's dawn,
Young and ould away we started
  Wid the basket and the slawn ;
But the heart within the bosom
  Gave one leap of awful dread
At each darlin' pratee blossom,
  White and purple, lyin' dead.
Down we dug, but only scattered
  Poisoned spuds along the slope ;
Though each ridge in vain it flattered
  Our poor hearts' revivin' hope.

But the desperate toil we'd double
　　On into the evenin' shades ;
Till the earth to share our trouble
　　Shook beneath our groanin' spades ;
Till a mist across the meadows
　　From the graveyard rose and spread,
And 'twas rumoured ghostly shadows,
　　Phantoms of our fathers dead,
Moved among us, wildly sharin'
　　In the women's sobs and sighs,
And our stony, still despairin',
　　Till night covered up the skies.

Thin we knew for bitter certain
　　That the vinom-breathin' cloud,
Closin' still its cruel curtain,
　　Surely yet would be our shroud.
And the fearful sights did folly,
　　Och ! no voice could rightly tell,
But that constant, melancholy
　　Murmur of the passin' bell ;
Till to toll it none among us
　　Strong enough at last was found,
And a silence overhung us
　　Awfuller nor any sound.

THE HOUR WE PARTED.

THE hour we parted,
When broken-hearted
You clung around me,
   Maureen, aroo,*
I swore I'd treasure,
Thro' pain and pleasure,
Thro' health and sickness,
   My love for you.

And still that jewel,
Thro' changes cruel
Of fickle Fortune
   I'll jealous guard;
Still let her vary,
The jade contràry,
If but my Mary
   Be my reward.

Yes! scorn and anger,
Distress and languor,
They're welcome willing,
   The long day thro',

---
* My grief.

Could I feel certain
The ev'ning's curtain
But clos'd us nearer,
   Maureen, aroo.

The dreamy shadows
Along the meadows
Go softly stealing,
   And falls the dew;
And o'er the billows,
Like faithful swallows,
All, all my thoughts, dear,
   Fly home to you.

With touches silken,
I see you milkin'
The crossest Kerry
   In Adragole;
And like a fairy,
You're singing, Mary,
Till every keeler
   Is foaming full.

The night is falling,
And you are calling

The cattle homeward
With coaxing tone ;
In God's own keeping,
Awake or sleeping,
'Tis now I leave you,
Maureen, mavrone ! *

THE IRISH EXILE'S LOVE.

WITH pensive eyes she passed the church,
And up the leafy woodland came ;
Until she reached the silver birch
Where long ago he carved her name.

And " Oh ! " she sighed, as soft she kissed
With loving lips that gentle tree,
" Alone, alone, I keep the tryst,
Return to Ireland, love, and me.

" Return ! Columbia's realm afar,
Where year by year your feet delay,
We cannot match for moon or star
By silver night or golden day ;

---

* Term of endearment,

"Her birds are brighter far of wing,
 A richer lustre lights her flowers ;
Yet still they say no bird can sing
 Or blossom breathe as sweet as ours.

"Return ! Her levin-flashes dire
 Affright not here. We never know
Her awful rushing prairie fire,
 The silent horror of her snow.

"Return ! Her heart is wise and bold,
 Her borders beautiful and free,
Yet still the New is not the Old,
 Return to Ireland, love, and me."

THE FOGGY DEW.

OH ! a wan cloud was drawn
O'er the dim, weeping dawn,
As to Shannon's side I returned at last ;
And the heart in my breast
For the girl I loved best

Was beating—ah, beating, how loud and fast !
    While the doubts and the fears
    Of the long, aching years
Seemed mingling their voices with the moaning flood ;
    Till full in my path,
    Like a wild water-wraith,
My true love's shadow lamenting stood.

    But the sudden sun kissed
    The cold, cruel mist
Into dancing showers of diamond dew ;
    The dark flowing stream
    Laughed back to his beam,
And the lark soared singing aloft in the blue ;
    While no phantom of night,
    But a form of delight
Ran with arms outspread to her darling boy :
    And the girl I love best
    On my wild, throbbing breast
Hid her thousand treasures, with a cry of joy.

FIXIN' THE DAY.

PATRICK.

Arrah, answer me now, sweet Kitty Mulreddin,
Why won't you be fixin' the day of our weddin'?

KITTY.

Now, Patrick O'Brien, what a hurry you're in!
Can't you wait till the summer comes round to begin?

PATRICK.

O no, Kitty machree, in all sinse and all raison,
The winter's the properest marryin' saison;
For to comfort oneself from the frost and the rain,
There's nothin' like weddin' in winter, 'tis plain.

KITTY.

If it's only protection you want from the cowld,
There's a parish that's called the Equator, I'm tould,
That for single young men is kept hot through the year.
Where's the use of your marryin'? off wid you there!

PATRICK.

But there's also a spot not so pleasantly warmed,
Set aside for ould maids, if I'm rightly informed,

Where some mornin' if still she can't make up her mind,
A misfortunate colleen, called Kathleen, you'll find.

KITTY.

Is it threatenin' you are that I'll die an ould maid,
Who refused, for your sake, Mr. Laurence M'Quaide?
Faix! I think I'll forgive him ; for this I'll be bound,
He'd wait like a lamb till the summer came round.

PATRICK.

Now it's thinkin' I am that this same Mr. Larry
Is what makes you so slow in agreein' to marry.

KITTY.

And your wish to be settled wid *me* in such haste
Doesn't prove that you're jealous of *him* in the laste?

PATRICK.

Well, we'll not say that Kitty'll die an ould maid

KITTY.

And we'll bother no more about Larry M'Quaide.

PATRICK.

But, Kitty machree, sure those weddin's in spring,
When the Long Fast is out, are as common a thing

As the turfs in a rick, or the stones on a wall,—
Faith! you might just as well not be married at all.
But a weddin', consider, at this side of Lent,
Would be thought such a far more surprisin' event,—
So delightful to all at this dull time of year.
Now say "Yes!" for the sake of the neighbours, my dear!

KITTY.

No, Patrick, we'll wed when the woods and the grass
Wave a welcome of purtiest green, as we pass
Through the sweet cowslip meadow, and up by the mill
To the chapel itself on the side of the hill,—
Where the thorn, that's now sighin' a widow's lamint,
In a bridesmaid's costume 'll be smilin' contint,
And the thrush and the blackbird pipe, "Haste to the weddin',
Of Patrick O'Brien and Kitty Mulreddin."

PATRICK.

Will you really promise that, Kitty, you rogue?

KITTY.

Whisper, Patrick, The contract I'll seal wid—*a pogue.*
                                           [*Kissing him.*

MOLLEEN OGE.

Molleen oge, my Molleen oge,*
Go put on your natest brogue,
And slip into your smartest gown,
   You rosy little rogue;
   For a message kind I bear
   To yourself from ould Adair,
That Pat the piper's come around,
   And there'll be dancin' there.
      Oh, my Molleen,
      Oh, my colleen,
      We'll dance to Pat,
      And after that,
Collogue upon one chair.

   Molleen dear, I'd not presume
   To encroach into your room,
But I'd forgot a farin'
   I've brought you from Macroom;
   So open, and I swear
   Not one peep upon you; there!

---

* Young.

'Tis a silver net to gather
    At the glass your goolden hair.
        Oh, my Molleen,
        Oh, my colleen,
        We'll dance to Pat,
        And after that,
    Collogue upon one chair.

Molleen pet, my Molleen pet,
    Faix, I'm fairly in a fret
At the time you're tittivatin';
    Molleen, aren't you ready yet?
    Now net and gown and brogue,
    Are you sure you're quite the vogue?
But, bedad, you look so lovely,
    I'll forgive you, Molleen oge.
        Oh, my Molleen,
        Oh, my colleen,
        We'll dance to Pat,
        And after that,
    Upon one chair collogue.

IRISH LULLABY.

I'D rock my own sweet childie to rest in a cradle of gold on a bough of the willow,
To the *shoheen ho* of the wind of the west and the *lulla lo* of the soft sea billow.
  Sleep, baby dear,
  Sleep without fear,
Mother is here beside your pillow.

I'd put my own sweet childie to sleep in a silver boat on the beautiful river,
Where a *shoheen* whisper the white cascades, and a *lulla lo* the green flags shiver.
  Sleep, baby dear,
  Sleep without fear,
Mother is here with you for ever.

Lulla lo ! to the rise and fall of mother's bosom 'tis sleep has bound you,
And O, my child, what cosier nest for rosier rest could love have found you?
  Sleep, baby dear,
  Sleep without fear,
Mother's two arms are clasped around you.

THE MILL SONG.

Corn is a-sowing
  Over the hill,
The stream is a-flowing,
  Round goes the mill.

    Winding and grinding,
      Round goes the mill:
    Winding and grinding
      Should never stand still.
    The hands that are strongest
      Are welcome here,
    And those that work longest
      Earn the best cheer.

The green corn is hinting
  Over the hill,
Lasses tormenting
  The lads to their fill.

    Winding and grinding, etc.

The gold corn is glinting
  Over the hill;

Lasses consenting,
    Lads have their will.

    Winding and grinding, etc.

Corn is a-carrying
    Into the mill,
Young folk are marrying
    Over the hill.

    Winding and grinding, etc.

From the hands of the shaker
    Again goes the corn,
The old to God's acre
    Gently are borne.

    Winding and grinding, etc.

The green corn is glistening
    Once more with the spring;
Children are christening,
    Glad mothers sing.

    Winding and grinding, etc.

Thus our life runs around,
    Like the mill with its corn,

Young folk are marrying,
Old folk are burying,
  Young folk are born.

Winding and grinding,
  Round goes the mill;
Winding and grinding
  Should never stand still.
The hands that are strongest
  Are welcome here,
And they that work longest
  Earn the best cheer.

THE LITTLE RED LARK.

O<small>H</small>, swan of slenderness,
Dove of tenderness,
  Jewel of joys, arise!
The little red lark
 Like a rosy spark
  Of song to his sunburst flies.
But till thou art risen,
Earth is a prison
  Full of my lonesome sighs;

Then awake and discover
To thy fond lover
   The morn of thy matchless eyes.

The dawn is dark to me,
Hark! oh, hark to me,
   Pulse of my heart, I pray!
And out of thy hiding
With blushes gliding
   Dazzle me with thy day.
Ah, then, once more to thee
Flying, I'll pour to thee
   Passion so sweet and gay,
The lark shall listen,
And dewdrops glisten,
   Laughing on every spray.

LOVE'S WISHES.

WOULD I were Erin's apple blossom o'er you,
   Or Erin's rose in all its beauty blown,
To drop my richest petals down before you,
   Within the garden where you walk alone.

In hope you'll turn and pluck a little posy,
    With loving fingers through my foliage pressed,
And kiss it close and set it blushing rosy,
    To sigh out all its sweetness on your breast.

Would I might take the pigeon's flight towards you,
    And perch beside your window-pane above,
And murmur how my heart of hearts it hoards you,
    O hundred thousand treasures of my love;
In hope you'd stretch your slender hand and take me,
    And smooth my wildly fluttering wings to rest,
And lift me to your loving lips and make me
    My bower of blisses in your loving breast.

A LAMENTATION.

COLD, dark, and dumb lies my boy on his bed;
Cold, dark, and silent the night dews are shed;
Hot, swift, and fierce fall my tears for the dead!

His footprints lay light in the dew of the dawn
As the straight, slender track of the young mountain fawn;
But I'll ne'er again follow them over the lawn.

His manly cheek blushed with the sun's rising ray,
And he shone in his strength like the sun at midday;
But a cloud of black darkness has hid him away.

And that black cloud for ever shall cling to the skies:
And never, ah, never, I'll see him arise,
Lost warmth of my bosom, lost light of my eyes!

THE BANKS OF THE DAISIES.

When first I saw young Molly
Stretched beneath the holly
Fast asleep, forenint her sheep, one dreamy summer's day,
With daisies laughing round her
Hand and foot I bound her,
Then kissed her on her blooming cheek, and softly stole away.

But, as with blushes burning
Tip-toe I was turning,
From sleep she starts, and on me darts a dreadful lightning ray;
My foolish flowery fetters
Scornfully she scatters,
And like a winter sunbeam she coldly sweeps away.

> But Love, young Love, comes stooping
> O'er my daisies drooping,
>
> And oh! each flower with fairy power the rosy boy renews;
>
> Then twines each charming cluster
> In links of starry lustre,
>
> And with the chain enchanting my colleen proud pursues.

> And soon I met young Molly
> Musing melancholy
>
> With downcast eyes and starting sighs, along the meadow bank;
>
> And oh! her swelling bosom
> Was wreathed with daisy blossom,
>
> Like stars in summer heaven, as in my arms she sank.

THE ROSE-TREE IN FULL BEARING.

AN IRISH MELODY.

> O ROSE-TREE in full bearing,
> When rude storms had stripped the bowers,
> How oft, with thee despairing,
> I've sighed through the long dark hours!

Till Spring, so hard of wooing,
    Hope's own green spell upon thee cast,
And Kate, her coldness rueing,
    With sweet pity turned at last.

Then April smiled to cheer us,
    Or mocked grief with golden rain,
While Kate drew laughing near us,
    Or frowned past with dear disdain;
'Till, was it yester even?—
    Beneath thy faint red flowers divine,
With Love's one star in heaven,
    Her lips leant at last to mine!

And when I fondly told her,
    O Rose, all our stormy grief;
And how my hope grew bolder
    With thy every opening leaf;
She answered, "For so sharing,
    Dear heart, Love's weary winter hour,
The Rose-tree in full bearing
    Shall build us our summer bower."

HERRING IS KING.

Let all the fish that swim the sea,
   Salmon and turbot, cod and ling,
Bow down the head and bend the knee
   To herring, their king! to herring, their king!

Sing, Hugamar féin an sowra lin',
'Tis we have brought the summer in.*

The sun sank down so round and red
   Upon the bay, upon the bay;
The sails shook idly overhead,
   Becalmed we lay, becalmed we lay;

Sing, Hugamar féin an sowra lin',
'Tis we have brought the summer in.

Till Shawn the eagle dropped on deck,
   The bright-eyed boy, the bright-eyed boy;
'Tis he has spied your silver track,
   Herring, our joy, herring, our joy;

Sing, Hugamar féin an sowra lin',
'Tis we have brought the summer in.

---

* The second line of the refrain translates the first.

It was in with the sails and away to shore,
  With the rise and swing, the rise and swing
Of two stout lads at each smoking oar,
  After herring, our king, herring, our king;

Sing, Hugamar féin an sowra lin',
'Tis we have brought the summer in.

The Manx and the Cornish raised the shout,
  And joined the chase, and joined the chase,
But their fleets they fouled as they went about,
  And we won the race, we won the race;

Sing, Hugamar féin an sowra lin',
'Tis we have brought the summer in.

For we turned and faced you full to land,
  Down the góleen long, the góleen * long,
And after you slipped from strand to strand
  Our nets so strong, our nets so strong;

Sing, Hugamar féin an sowra lin',
'Tis we have brought the summer in.

Then we called to our sweathearts and our wives,
  "Come welcome us home, welcome us home,"

---

* Creek.

Till they ran to meet us for their lives
    Into the foam, into the foam ;

Sing, Hugamar féin an sowra lin',
'Tis we have brought the summer in.

O the kissing of hands and waving of caps
    From girl and boy, from girl and boy,
While you leapt by scores in the lasses' laps,
    Herring, our joy, herring, our joy ;

Sing, Hugamar féin an sowra lin',
'Tis we have brought the summer in.

MY LOVE'S AN ARBUTUS.

My love's an arbutus
By the borders of Lene,*
So slender and shapely
In her girdle of green
And I measure the pleasure
Of her eye's sapphire sheen

---

* Killarney.

By the blue skies that sparkle
Through that soft branching screen.

But though ruddy the berry
And snowy the flower,
That brighten together
The arbutus bower,
Perfuming and blooming
Through sunshine and shower,
Give *me* her bright lips
And her laugh's pearly dower.

Alas! fruit and blossom
Shall scatter the lea,
And Time's jealous fingers
Dim your young charms, Machree.
But unranging, unchanging,
You'll still cling to me,
Like the evergreen leaf
To the arbutus tree.

THE BLUE, BLUE SMOKE.

Oh, many and many a time
   In the dim old days,
When the chapel's distant chime
   Pealed the hour of evening praise,
I've bowed my head in prayer;
   Then shouldered scythe or bill,
And travelled free of care
   To my home across the hill;
     Whilst the blue, blue smoke
     Of my cottage in the coom,
       Softly wreathing,
       Sweetly breathing,
     Waved my thousand welcomes home.

For oft and oft I've stood,
   Delighted in the dew,
Looking down across the wood,
   Where it stole into my view—
Sweet spirit of the sod,
   Of our own Irish earth,

Going gently up to God
  From the poor man's hearth.
    O, the blue, blue smoke,
    Of my cottage in the coom,
      Softly wreathing,
      Sweetly breathing
    My thousand welcomes home.

But I hurried swiftly on,
  When Herself from the door
Came swimming like a swan
  Beside the Shannon shore;
And after her in haste,
  On pretty, pattering feet,
Our rosy cherubs raced
  Their daddy dear to meet;
    While the blue, blue smoke
    Of my cottage in the coom,
      Softly wreathing,
      Sweetly breathing,
    Waved my thousand welcomes home.

But the times are sorely changed
  Since those dim old days,

And far, far I've ranged
   From those dear old ways;
And my colleen's golden hair
   To silver all has grown,
And our little cherub pair
   Have cherubs of their own;
      And the black, black smoke,
      Like a heavy funeral plume,
         Darkly wreathing,
         Fearful breathing,
      Crowns the city with its gloom.

But 'tis our comfort sweet
   Through the long toil of life,
That we'll turn with tired feet
   From the noise and the strife,
And wander slowly back
   In the soft western glow,
Hand in hand by the track
   That we trod long ago;
      Till the blue, blue smoke
      Of our cottage in the coom,
         Softly wreathing,
         Sweetly breathing,
      Waves our thousand welcomes home.

'TWAS PRETTY TO BE IN BALLINDERRY.

'TWAS pretty to be in Ballinderry,
   'Twas pretty to be in Aghalee,
'Twas prettier to be in little Ram's Island,
   Trysting under the ivy tree !
      Ochone, ochone !
      Ochone, ochone !
For often I roved in little Ram's Island,
Side by side with Phelimy Hyland,
And still he'd court me and I'd be coy,
Though at heart I loved him, my handsome boy !

" I'm going," he sighed, "from Ballinderry
   Out and across the stormy sea ;
Then if in your heart you love me, Mary,
   Open your arms at last to me."
      Ochone, ochone !
      Ochone, ochone !
I opened my arms; how well he knew me !
I opened my arms and took him to me ;

And there, in the gloom of the groaning mast,
We kissed our first and we kissed our last!

'Twas happy to be in little Ram's Island,
    But now 'tis sad as sad can be ;
For the ship that sailed with Phelimy Hyland,
    It sunk for ever beneath the sea.
        Ochone, ochone!
        Ochone, ochone!
And 'tis oh ! but I wear the weeping willow,
And wander alone by the lonesome billow,
And cry to him over the cruel sea,
"Phelimy Hyland, come back to me !"

O THOU OF THE BEAUTIFUL HAIR.

OF all the girls with clustering curls from Kerry to Kildare,
There's not a lass that can surpass my love with the golden hair.
Oh ! if the sun should cease to shine, the moon refused her ray,
Her very shadow on the earth would turn the night to day.

Now what's my chance to gain a glance from one so good and fair,
With all the boys from Clanmacnoise to Cork around her chair?
Yet somehow still she steals one look upon me through the throng;
And when I sing, with smiles and tears she answers to my song.

MOLLY HEWSON.

Molly bawn,* white as lawn,
    Rosy as the rowan † spray,
Had us all in her thrall,
    Young and old, and grave and gay;
For her glances through the dances
    Such fond fancies o'er us shed,
None felt sure he struck the floor
    With his heels or with his head.

Molly bawn, white as lawn,
    Sweeter than the sugar-cane,

---

* Fair.   † Mountain Ash.

Drops her eyes at the boys,
   Never glancing back again.
Some say shyness 'tis, or coyness,
   And 'tis fineness some believe;
But at all, great and small,
   I'm just laughing in my sleeve.

For there's none 'neath the sun
   But myself could tell you why
Molly seems lost in dreams,
   When the saucy lads go by.
But that reason out of season
   'Twould be treason now to show;
After Lent I'm content
   Father Tom and all should know.

THE CONFESSION.

A LOVELY lass with modest mien
   Stole out one morning early;
The dew-drops glancing o'er the green
   Made all her pathway pearly.

THE CONFESSION.

Young Lawrence struck with Cupid's dart,—
    Cupid's dart distressing,—
As through the fields he saw her start,
    Sighed, "She's gone confessing !
O vo ! 'twould ease *my* heart
    To earn the Father's blessing."

The Father, with a twinkling eye,
    He watched my boyo cunning,
Unnoticed by his colleen's eye,
    Behind the bushes running.
"How well," he laughed, "young Lawrence there,
    After all my pressing,
With his sweetheart, I declare,
    Comes at last confessing.
Oho ! I'll just take care
    To learn the lad a lesson."

The pleasant priest unbarred the door,
    As solemn as a shadow,
"How slow," cried he, "you've come before,
    How hot-foot now, my laddo.
The serious steal with looks sedate,
    Seeking to be shriven,

But you, you're in no fitting state
   Now to be forgiven,
So go within and wait,
   With all your thoughts on heaven."

The fair one following in a while
   Made out her faults with meekness;
The priest then asked her with a smile
   Had she no other weakness,
And led with that young Lawrence in;
   Her cheeks were now confessing.
"Well, since 'tis after all a sin
   Easy of redressing,
Here, dear, I'd best begin
   To give you both my blessing."

WITH THE NORTH.

With lip contemptuous curling,
   She cried, "Is freedom's flag above
Fold on fold unfurling,
   And Patrick pleading love?

Oh! yes, when patriots hand in hand
Unite to free their foster-land
From slavery's accursed band,
   What true man woos a woman?
Then, with my bitter scorning,
   Go, live dishonoured, die a slave,
Or march to-morrow morning
   To battle with the brave."

"We'll steal a march on sorrow,"
   Our Captain sighed, a soldier grey;
"Sound the drum to-morrow
   Before the dawn of day."
But ere the drum's first muffled beat,
The women crowded down the street,
How many never more to meet
   Their death-devoted heroes.
Then as I passed her dwelling,
   My proud one o'er her casement frame,
The sobs her bosom swelling,
   Leant forth and sighed my name.

Oh! have you seen Atlantic
   Advance his green, resistless line

Against the cliffs gigantic,
    And bury them in brine?
Thus on our stubborn foe we fell,
Death's lightning darting from our steel,
Whilst round us every cannon peal
    A hero's requiem thundered!
And still with forward faces
    Went down in death our dauntless men,
And still into their places
    As gallant hearts stepped in.

Till to a sunburst glorious,
    That all the field of battle fired,
Before our van victorious
    The sullen South retired.
Then peace returned, and from the war
Our banner bright with many a star
'Twas mine to flutter from afar
    In triumph to our city;
Till I at last could wreathe it
    Around my true love's throbbing heart,
And we two kissed beneath it,
    Oh! never more to part.

THE POTATO BLOSSOM.

As fiddle in hand
I crossed the land,
Wid homesick heart so weighty,
I chanced to meet
A girl so sweet
That she turned my grief to gai'ty.
Now what cause for pause
Had her purty feet?
Faix, the beautiful flower of the pratee.

Then more power to the flower of the pratee,
The beautiful flower of the pratee,
For fixin' the feet
Of that colleen sweet,
On the road to Cincinnati.

You'd imagine her eye
Was a bit of blue sky,
And her cheek had a darlin' dimple.

Her footstep faltered;
She blushed, and altered
Her shawl wid a timid trimble.
And, "oh, sir, what's the blossom
You wear on your bosom?"
She asked most sweet and simple.

I looked in her face
To see could I trace
Any hint of lurkin' levity;
But there wasn't a line
Of her features fine
But expressed the gentlest gravity.
So quite at my aise
At her innocent ways,
Wid sorra a sign of brevity,

Says I, "Don't you know
Where these blossoms blow,
And their name of fame, mavourneen? *
I'd be believin'
You were deceivin'
Shiel Dhuv this summer mornin',

---

* My dear.

If your eyes didn't shine
So frank on mine,
Such a schemin' amusement scornin'.

Now I don't deny
'Twould be asy why,
Clane off widout any reflection—
Barely to name
The plant of fame
Whose flower is your eyes' attraction;
Asy for me,
But to you, machree,
Not the slenderest satisfaction;

For somehow I know
If I answered you so,
You'd be mad you could disrimimber
In what garden or bower
You'd seen this flower,
Or adornin' what forest timber,
Or where to seek
For its fruit unique
From June until Novimber.

Since thin, I reply,
You take such joy
In this blossom I love so dearly,
Wid a bow like this
Shall I lave you, miss,
Whin I've mentioned the name of it merely;
Or take your choice,
Wid music and voice,
Shall I sing you its history clearly?"

"Oh, the song, kind sir,
I'd much prefer,"
She answered wid eager gai'ty.
So we two and the fiddle
Turned off from the middle
Of the road to Cincinnati,
And from under the shade
That the maples made
I sang her—

THE SONG OF THE PRATEE.

When after the Winter alarmin',
The Spring steps in so charmin',

So fresh and arch
In the middle of March,
Wid her hand St. Patrick's arm on,
Let us all, let us all be goin',
Agra, to assist at your sowin',
The girls to spread
Your iligant bed,
And the boys to set the hoe in.

CHORUS,—

Then good speed to your seed! God's grace and increase.
Never more in our need may you blacken wid the blight;
But when Summer is o'er in our gardens, astore,*
May the fruit at your root fill our bosoms wid delight.

So rest and sleep, my jewel,
Safe from the tempest cruel;
Till violets spring
And skylarks sing
From Mourne to Carran Tual.
Then wake and build your bower
Through April sun and shower,
To bless the earth
That gave you birth,
Through many a sultry hour.

---

* A term of affection.

CHORUS,—

Then good luck to your leaf. And ochone, ologone,
  Never more to our grief may it blacken wid the blight,
But when Summer is o'er·in our gardens, astore,
  May the fruit at your root fill our bosoms wid delight.

   Thus smile with glad increasin',
   Till to St. John we're raisin'
     Through Erin's isle
     The pleasant pile
   That sets the bonfire blazin'.
   O 'tis then that the Midsummer fairy,
   Abroad on his sly vagary,
     Wid purple and white,
     As he passes by night,
   Your emerald leaf shall vary.

CHORUS,—

Then more power to your flower, and your merry green leaf
  Never more to our grief may they blacken wid the blight
But when Summer is o'er, in our gardens, astore,
  May the fruit at your root fill our bosoms wid delight.

   And once again, Mavourneen,
   Some mellow Autumn mornin',

At red sunrise
Both girls and boys
To your garden ridge we're turnin',
Then under your foliage fadin'
Each man of us sets his spade in,
While the colleen bawn
Her brown kishane *
Full up wid your fruit is ladin'.

CHORUS,—

Then good luck to your leaf! more power to your flower!
Never more to our grief may they blacken wid the blight;
But when Summer is o'er, in our gardens, astore,
May the fruit at your root fill our bosoms wid delight.

Then we rose, we two,
In dread of the dew,
And she blushed to her beautiful bosom,
As soft she said,
"Now I'll never forget
This flower's the Potato Blossom."

---

* A large basket carried upon the back.

MAUREEN, MAUREEN.

Oh ! Maureen, Maureen, have you forgotten
    The fond confession that you made to me,
While round us fluttered the white bog cotton,
    And o'er us waved the wild arbutus tree?
Like bits of sky bo-peeping through the bower,
    No sooner were your blue eyes sought than flown,
Till white and fluttering as the cotton flower
    Your slender hand it slipped into my own.

Oh ! Maureen, Maureen, do you remember
    The faithful promise that you pledged to me
The night we parted in black December
    Beneath the tempest-tossed arbutus tree,
When faster than the drops from heaven flowing,
    Your heavy tears they showered with ceaseless start,
And wilder than the storm-wind round us blowing,
    Your bitter sobs they smote upon my heart?

Oh ! Maureen, Maureen, for your love only
    I left my father and mother dear;

Within the churchyard they're lying lonely,
  'Tis from their tombstone I've travelled here.
Their only son, you sent me o'er the billow,
  Ochone! though kneeling they implored me stay;
They sickened, with no child to smooth their pillow;
  They died. Are you as dead to me as they?

Oh! Maureen, must then the love I bore you—
  Seven lonesome summers of longing trust—
Turn like the fortune I've gathered for you,
  Like treacherous fairy treasure, all to dust?
But Maureen bawn asthore, your proud lips quiver;
  Into your scornful eyes the tears they start;
Your rebel hand returns to mine for ever;
  Oh! Maureen, Maureen, never more we'll part.

ONE SUNDAY AFTER MASS.

    One Sunday after Mass,
    As Lawrence and his lass
    Through the green woods did pass
    All alone and all alone,
Chorus.—*All alone, and all alone!*

He asked her for a pogue,
But she called him a rogue,
And she beat him with her brogue,*
Ochone and ochone,

CHORUS.—*Ochone and ochone!*

At first my boy he bent,
As if to take, content,
His proper punishment.
Small blame too, small blame!

CHORUS.—*Small blame too, small blame!*

But on her purty foot,
Unbothered by a boot,
He pressed a warm salute.
For shame! fie! for shame!

CHORUS.—*For shame! fie! for shame.*

Then Larry gets the worst,
For she boxed his ears at first,
Then into tears she burst,
Ochone and ochone.

CHORUS.—*Ochone and ochone!*

But soon the artful rogue
Soothed his crying colleen oge,

---

* Boot.

Till she gave him just one pogue,
   All alone, and all alone !

CHORUS.—*All alone, and all alone !*

WHEN I ROSE IN THE MORNING.

WHEN I rose in the morning,
   My heart full of woe,
I implored all the song birds
   Why their mates on the bough
To their pleading gave heeding,
   While Kate still said "No";
But they made no kind answer
   To a heart full of woe.

Till the wood-quest at noon
   From the forest below
He taught me his secret
   So tender and low,
Of stealing fond feeling
   With sweet notes of woe,

Coo-cooing so soft
　　　　Through the green, leafy row.

　　Then the long shadows fell,
　　　And the sun he sank low,
　　And again I was pleading
　　　In the mild evening glow:
　"Ah! Kitty, have pity!"
　　　Then how could she say "No."
　So for ever I'm free
　　　From that heart full of woe.

THE GIRL I LEFT BEHIND ME.

　　The route has come, we march away,
　　　Our colours dance before us,
　　But sorrow's cloud made dark the day
　　　That from our sweethearts tore us;
　　My own dear lass she sobbed "adieu,"
　　　Her loving arms entwined me,
　　And oft she prayed me to be true
　　　To the girl I left behind me.

THE GIRL I LEFT BEHIND ME.

Yes! I'll be true; when steel to steel
   The ranks of war are rolling,
And round us every cannon peal
   A funeral knell is tolling;
Then if from out the battle flame
   A fatal ball should find me,
My dying lips shall bless the name
   Of the girl I've left behind me.

But, if in triumph I return
   To tell a soldier's story,
Though proudly on my breast should burn
   Victoria's cross of glory,
No other maid with magic art
   Shall break the links that bind me
For ever to the faithful heart
   Of the girl I've left behind me.

THE SAILOR GIRL.

WHEN the Wild-Geese* were flying to Flanders away,
I clung to my Desmond, beseeching him stay,
But the stern trumpet sounded the summons to sea,
And afar the ship bore him, mabouchal machree.†

And first he sent letters, and then he sent none,
And three times into prison I dreamt he was thrown;
So I shore my long tresses, and stained my face brown,
And went for a sailor from Limerick town.

Oh! the ropes cut my fingers, but steadfast I strove,
Till I reached the Low Country in search of my love.
There I heard how at Namur his heart was so high,
That they carried him captive, refusing to fly.

With that to King William himself I was brought,
And his mercy for Desmond with tears I besought.

---

* The popular name given to the Irish who followed Sarsfield into the Low Countries after the Capitulation of Limerick.
† My heart's own boy.

He considered my story, then smiling, said he,
"The young Irish rebel for your sake is free.

"Bring the varlet before us. Now, Desmond O' Hea,
Myself has decided your sentence to-day.
You must marry your sailor with bell, book, and ring,
And here is her dowry," cried William the King!

JACK THE JOLLY PLOUGHBOY.

As Jack the jolly ploughboy was ploughing through the land,
He turned his share and shouted to bid his horses stand,
Then down beside his team he sat, contented as a king,
And Jack he sang his song so sweet he made the mountains ring

> *With his Ta-ran-nan nanty na,*
> *Sing ta-ran-nan nanty na,*
> *While the mountains all ringing re-echoed the singing*
> *Of Ta-ran-nan nanty na.*

'Tis said old England's sailors, when wintry tempests roar,
Will plough the stormy waters and pray for those on shore;

But through the angry winter the share, the share for me,
To drive a steady furrow, and pray for those at sea.

   With my Ta-ran-nan nanty na, etc.

When heaven above is bluest, and earth most green below,
Away from wife and sweetheart the fisherman must go;
But golden seed I'll scatter beside the girl I love,
And smile to hear the cuckoo, and sigh to hear the dove,

   With my Ta-ran-nan nanty na, etc.

'Tis oft the hardy fishers a scanty harvest earn,
And gallant tars from glory on wooden legs return,
But a bursting crop for ever shall dance before my flail,
For I'll live and die a farmer all in the Golden Vale.

   With my Ta-ran-nan nanty na, etc.

A LOVE SONG.

From the Celtic.

O Mary bawn asthore,
 That through my bosom's core
Hast pierced me past the Isle of Fōdla's * healing;
 By Heaven, 'tis my belief,
 Had you but known my grief,
Long since to me with succour you'd been stealing.

---

   * Ireland.

A LOVE SONG.

With tears the night I waste;
No food by day I taste,
But wander weak and silent as a shadow!
Ah! if I may not find
My Mary true and kind,
My mother soon must weep, a sonless widow.

I know not night from day:
"Cuckoo!" the thrushes say!
But how can it be May in dark December?
My friends look strange and wild;
But hasten, Mary mild,
And well my heart its mistress shall remember.

No herb or skill of hand
My cure can now command,
From you, O Flower of Love, alone I'll seek it;
Then hasten, hasten here,
My own and only dear,
And in your secret ear I'll softly speak it.

One sweet kiss from your mouth
Would quench my burning drouth,
And lift me back to life; ah! yield it to me;

  Or make for me my bed
  Among the mouldering dead,
Where the winding worms may crawl and channel through
   me.

  Ah! better buried so
  Than like a ghost to go,
All music, dance, and sport with sighs forsaking;
  A witless, wandering man
  For the love of Mary bawn,
With the heart within my bosom slowly breaking.

SPINNING-WHEEL SONG.

ONCE my wheel ran cheerily round,
 Ran cheerily round from day to day,
But now it drags how wearily round;
 For Owen's gone away.
Once I spun soft carolling O,
 Soft carolling O! from morn to eve,
But since we started quarrelling, oh!
 'Tis silently I weave.

Has he joined Sir Arthur, ochone!
    Sir Arthur, ochone! to fight the French?
Though he was rude, I'd rather, ochone!
    He joined me on this bench.
Hush! he's been deluthering you,
    Deluthering you with swords and drums,
And now I think 'tis soothering you,
    'Tis soothering you, he comes.

THE LIMERICK LASSES.

"Have you e'er a new song,
    My Limerick Poet,
To help us along
    Wid this terrible boat
Away over to Tork?"
"Arrah, I understand;
    For all of your work,
'Twill tighten you, boys,
    To cargo that sand
    To the overside strand,
      Wid the current so strong,
      Unless you've a song—
A song to lighten and brighten you, boys.

Be listenin' then,

My brave Kerry men,

And the new song,

And the true song

Of the Limerick Lasses 'tis I will begin."

O Limerick dear,

It's far and it's near

I've travelled the round of this circular sphere;

Still an' all to my mind,

No colleens you'll find

As lovely and modest, as merry and kind,

As our Limerick Lasses;

Our Limerick Lasses—

So lovely and modest, so merry and kind.

CHORUS.—*So row,*

Strong and slow,

Chorusing after me as we go,—

Still in all to my mind

No colleens you'll find,

As lovely and modest, as merry and kind,

As our Limerick Lasses,

Our Limerick Lasses,

So lovely and modest, so merry and kind.

O your English colleen
Has the wonderful mien
Of a goddess in marble, all grand and serene;
And, though slow to unbend,
Win her once for your friend,
And—no alter or falter—she's yours to the end.

CHORUS.—*But O! row,*
    Strong and slow,
Chorusing after me as we go,—etc.

Of the French demoiselle
Delighted I'll tell,
For her sparkle and grace suit us Irishmen well;
And, taken complete,
From her head to her feet,
She's the perfectest picture of polish you'll meet.

CHORUS.—*But O! row,*
    Strong and slow,
Chorusing after me as we go,—etc.

O, Donna of Spain,
It's the darlingest pain
From your dark eyes I've suffered again and again,

THE LIMERICK LASSES.

When you'd gracefully glide,
Like a swan at my side,
Or sing till with rapture the woodbird replied.

CHORUS.—*But O! row,*
Strong and slow,
Chorusing after me as we go,—etc.

Now my Maryland girl,
With your sunshiny curl,
Your sweet spirit eyes, and complexion of pearl;
And the goodness and grace,
That illumine your face,
You're the purtiest approach to my Limerick Lass.

CHORUS.—*For O! row,*
Strong and slow,
Chorusing after me as we go,—
Still an' all to my mind,
No maiden you'll find,
As lovely and modest, as merry and kind,
As our Limerick Lasses,
Our Limerick Lasses,
So lovely and modest, and merry and kind.

O'FARRELL THE FIDDLER.

Now, thin, what has become
   Of Thady O'Farrell?
The honest poor man,
   What's delayin' him, why?
O, the thrush might be dumb,
   And the lark cease to carol,
Whin his music began
   To comether * the sky.

Three summers have gone
   Since we've missed you, O'Farrell,
From the weddin' and patron †
   And fair on the green.
In an hour to St. John
   We'll light up the tar-barrel,
But ourselves we're not flatter'n'
   That thin you'll be seen.

O Thady, we've watched
   And we've waited for ever

---

* Put a spell upon.
† Festival of a Patron Saint, pronounced "pattern."

To see your ould self
 Steppin' into the town—
Wid your corduroys patched
 So clane and so clever,
And the pride of a Guelph
 In your smile or your frown—

Till some one used say,
 "Here's Thady O'Farrell;"
And "God bless the good man!
 Let's go meet him," we cried;
And wid this from their play,
 And wid that from their quarrel,
All the little ones ran
 To be first at your side.

Soon amongst us you'd stand,
 Wid the ould people's blessin',
As they lean'd from the door
 To look out at you pass;
Wid the colleen's kiss-hand,
 And the childer's caressin',
And the boys fightin', sure,
 Which'd stand your first glass.

Thin you'd give us the news
    Out of Cork and Killarney—
Had O'Flynn married yet?—
    Was ould Mack still at work?—
Shine's political views—
    Barry's last bit of blarney—
And the boys you had met
    On their way to New York.

And whin from the sight
    Of our say-frontin' village
The far frownin' Blasquet
    Stole into the shade,
And the warnin' of night
    Called up from the tillage
The girl wid her basket,
    The boy wid his spade—,

By the glowin' turf-fire,
    Or the harvest moon's glory,
In the close-crowded ring
    That around you we made,
We'd no other desire
    Than your heart-thrillin' story,

Or the song that you'd sing,
    Or the tune that you played.

Till you'd ax, wid a leap
    From your seat in the middle,
And a shuffle and slide
    Of your foot on the floor,
" Will we try a jig-step,
    Boys and girls, to the fiddle ? "
" Faugh a ballagh," * we cried,
    " For a jig to be sure."

For whinever you'd start
    Jig or planxty † so merry,
Wid their caperin' twirls
    And their rollickin' runs,
Where's the heel or the heart
    In the kingdom of Kerry
Of the boys and the girls
    Wasn't wid you at once ?

So you'd tune wid a sound
    That arose as delightin'

---

* Clear the way.   † A quick dance tune.

As our own colleen's voice,
   So sweet and so clear,
As she coyly wint round,
   Wid a curtsey invitin'
The best of the boys
   For the fun to prepare.

For a minute or so,
   Till the couples were ready,
On your shoulder and chin
   The fiddle lay quiet;
Then down came your bow
   So quick and so steady,
And away we *should* spin
   To the left or the right!

Thin how Micky Dease
   Forged * steps was a wonder,
And well might our women
   Of Roseen be proud—
Such a face, such a grace,
   And her darlin' feet under
Like two swallows skimmin'
   The skirts of a cloud.

---

* Invented new steps by continuing old ones.

Thin, Thady, ochone!
  Come back, for widout you
We are never as gay
  As we were in the past!

  * * * *

O Thady, mavrone,
  Why, thin, I wouldn't doubt you.
Huzzah! boys, huzzah!
  Here's O'Farrell at last!

LONESOME LOVERS.

SHE.

OCHONE! Patrick Blake,
  You're off up to Dublin,
And sure for your sake
  I'm the terrible trouble in;
For I thought that I knew
  What my "Yes" and my "No" meant,
Till I tried it on you
  That misfortunate moment.

CHORUS.—*But somehow I find,*
    Since I sent Pat away,
    Must be in my mind
    I was wishful he'd stay.

While ago the young rogue
    Came and softly stooped over,
And gave me a *pogue*
    As I stretched in the clover:
How I boxed his two ears,
    And axed him "How dare he?"
Now I'd let him for years—
    'Tis the way women vary;

CHORUS.—*For somehow I find,*
    Since I sent Pat away,
    Must be in my mind
    I was wishful he'd stay.

Oh, why wouldn't he wait
    To put his *comether* *
Upon me complete,
    When we both were together?
But no, Patrick, no;
    You must have me consentin'

---

* "Come hither!"

Too early, and so
    Kitty's late for repentin'.

CHORUS.—*For somehow I find,*
    Since I've sent Pat away,
  Must be in my mind
    I was wishful he'd stay.

HE.

Oh! Kitty O'Hea,
    I'm the terrible trouble in,
For you're at Rossbeigh
    And myself is in Dublin,
Through mistaking, bedad!
    Your blushes and that trick
Of sighing you had
    Showed a softness for Patrick;

CHORUS.—*And yet from my mind*
    A voice seems to speak:—
  "Go back, and you'll find
    That she's fond of you, Blake!"

Oh! Dublin is grand,
    As all must acknowledge,

Wid the Bank on one hand,
    On the other the College.
I'd be proud to be Mayor
    Of so splendid a city,
But I'd far sooner share
    A cabin wid Kitty;

CHORUS.—*And I may so some day,*
    For that voice in my mind
    Keeps seeming to say :—
        "After all she'll be kind."

Oh! Dublin is fine
    Wid her ships on the river,
And her iligant line
    Of bridges for ever.
But, Kitty, my dear,
    I'd exchange them this minute
For our small little pier
    And my boat, and you in it.

CHORUS.—*And I may so some day, etc.*

Here you've beautiful squares
    For all to be gay in,

Promenading in pairs,
   Wid the band music playin';
But if I'd my choice,
   Where our green hollies glisten,
To Kitty's sweet voice
   I'd far sooner listen.

CHORUS.—*And I may so some day*, *etc.*

Here's a wonderful Park,
   Where the wild beasts are feedin'
For the world like Noah's Ark
   Or the Garden of Eden!
But, faix! of the two,
   I'd rather be sittin'
Manœuv'ring, aroo!
   Wid your comical kitten.

CHORUS.—*And I may so some day*, *etc.*

Yes, Dublin's a Queen
   Wid her gardens and waters,
And her buildings between
   For her sons and her daughters;

In learning so great,
   So lovely and witty ;
But she isn't complate
   At all widout Kitty.

CHORUS.—*And that voice in my mind,—*
   " Go back to the South ! "—
So I will then, and find
   What you mane from her mouth.

THE WHITE BLOSSOM 'S OFF THE BOG.

THE white blossom 's off the bog, and the leaves are off the trees,
And the singing birds have scattered across the stormy seas ;
     And oh ! 'tis winter,
     Wild, wild winter !
With the lonesome wind sighing for ever through the trees.

How green the leaves were springing ! how glad the birds
    were singing !
When I rested in the meadow with my head on Patrick's
    knees ;
   And oh ! 'twas spring time,
   Sweet, sweet spring time !
With the daisies all dancing before in the breeze.

With the spring the fresh leaves they'll laugh upon the
    trees,
And the birds they'll flutter back with their songs across
    the seas,
But I'll never rest again with my head on Patrick's
    knees ;
   And for me 'twill be winter,
   All the year winter,
With the lonesome wind sighing for ever through the
    trees.

JENNY, I'M NOT JESTING.

"Ah, Jenny, I'm not jesting,
  Believe what I'm protesting,
  And yield what I'm requesting
      These seven years through."
"Ah, Lawrence, I may grieve you;
  Yet, if I can't relieve you,
  Sure, why should I deceive you
      With words untrue?
  But, since you must be courtin',
  There's Rosy and her fortune,
  'Tis rumoured you're consortin'
      With her of late.
  Or there's your cousin Kitty,
  So charming and so witty,
  She'd wed you out of pity,
      Kind Kate."

"Fie! Jenny, since I knew you,
  Of all the lads that woo you,

None's been so faithful to you,
 If truth were told:
Even when yourself was dartin'
Fond looks at fickle Martin,
Till off the thief went startin'
 For Sheela's gold."

" And if you've known me longest,
 Why should your love be strongest,
 And his that's now the youngest,
 For that be worst?"

" Fire, Jenny, quickest kindled
 Is always soonest dwindled,
 And thread the swiftest spindled
 Snaps first."

" If that's your wisdom, Larry,
 The longer I can tarry,
 The luckier I shall marry
 At long, long last."

" I've known of girls amusing
 Their minds, the men refusing,
 Till none were left for choosing
 At long, long last."

" Well, since it seems that marriage
 Is still the safest carriage,

And all the world disparage
    The spinster lone ;
Since you might still forsake me,
I think I'll let you take me,
Yes ! Larry, you may make me
    Your own !"

ANCIENT LULLABY.

O SLEEP, my baby, you are sharing
With the sun in rest repairing ;
While the moon her silver chair in
    Watches with your mother.
Shoheen, sho lo,
Lulla lo lo ! *

The morning on a bed of roses,
Evening on rude hills reposes :

---

* Irish hush words.

ANCIENT LULLABY.

Dusk his heavy eyelid closes,
   Under dreamy curtains.
Shoheen, sho lo,
Lulla lo lo !

The winds lie lulled on bluest billows,
Shining stars on cloudy pillows,
Waters under nodding willows,
   Mists upon the mountains.
Shoheen, sho lo,
Lulla lo lo !

Upon the fruits, upon the flowers,
On the wood birds in their bowers,
On low huts and lofty towers,
   Blessed sleep has fallen.
Shoheen, sho lo,
Lulla lo lo !

And ah ! my child as free from cumber,
Thus thro' life could'st thou but slumber,
Thus in death go join the number
   Of God's smiling angels.
Shoheen sho lo,
Lulla lo lo !

THE FOX HUNT.

THE first morning of March in the year '33,
There was frolic and fun in our own country;
The King's County Hunt over meadows and rocks,
Most nobly set out in the search of a fox.

Hullahoo! harkaway! hullahoo! harkaway!
Hullahoo! harkaway, boys! away, harkaway!

When they started bold Reynard he faced Tullamore,
Through Wicklow and Arklow along the sea-shore;
There he brisked up his brush with a laugh, and says he,
"'Tis mighty refreshing this breeze from the sea."

Hullahoo! harkaway! hullahoo! harkaway!
Hullahoo! harkaway, boys! away, harkaway!

With the hounds at his heels every inch of the way,
He led us by sunset right into Roscrea;
Here he ran up a chimney and out of the top
The rogue he cried out for the hunters to stop

From their loud harkaway! hullahoo! harkaway!
Hullahoo! harkaway, boys! away, harkaway!

"'Twas a long thirsty stretch since we left the sea-shore,
But, lads, here you've gallons of claret galore;
Myself will make free just to slip out of view,
And take a small pull at my own mountain dew."

So no more hullahoo! hullahoo! harkaway!
Hullahoo! harkaway, boys! away harkaway!

One hundred and twenty good sportsmen went down,
And sought him from Ballyland through Ballyboyne;
We swore that we'd watch him the length of the night,
So Reynard, sly Reynard, lay hid till the light.

Hullahoo! harkaway! hullahoo! harkaway!
Hullahoo! harkaway, boys! away, harkaway!

But the hills they re-echoed right early next morn
With the cry of the hounds and the call of the horn,
And in spite of his action, his craft, and his skill,
Our fine fox was taken on top of the hill.

Hullahoo! harkaway! hullahoo! harkaway!
Hullahoo! harkaway, boys! away, harkaway!

When Reynard he knew that his death was so nigh,
For pen, ink and paper he called with a sigh:

And all his dear wishes on earth to fulfil,
With these few dying words he declared his last will,

While we ceased harkaway! hullahoo! harkaway!
Hullahoo! harkaway, boys! away, harkaway!

"Here's to you, Mr. Casey, my Curraghmore estate,
And to you, young O'Brien, my money and plate,
And to you, Thomas Dennihy, my whip, spurs, and cap,
For no leap was so cross that you'd look for a gap."

And of what he made mention they found it no blank,
For he gave them a cheque on the National Bank.

COLLEEN OGE ASTHORE.

WHEN I marched away to war,
How you kissed me o'er and o'er;
Weeping, pressed me;
Sobbing, blessed me;
Colleen, colleen oge asthore.

I was wounded, wounded sore,
Dead, your father falsely swore;
 Mad to harry
 You to marry
One with miser-gold in store.

Ah! but when you dreamed me dead,
Forth you flew a wildered maid:
 Ever grieving,
 Ever weaving
Willow, willow for your head.

" Nay, he lives," your mother said,
But you only shook your head;
 " Why deceive me?
 Ah! believe me,
Mother, mother, he is dead."

So you pined and pined away,
Till, when in the winter grey
 Home I hasted,
 Wan and wasted,
Colleen, colleen oge, you lay.

"'Tis his lonesome ghost," you said,
"Come to call me to the dead;"
    "Nay, discover
    Your dear lover
Longing now at last to wed."

Then your cheek, so pale before,
With the rose of hope once more,
    Faintly, slowly,
    Brightly, wholly,
Blossomed, colleen oge asthore.

Till upon the chapel floor,
Side by side we knelt and swore
    Duty dearest,
    Love sincerest,
Colleen, colleen oge asthore.

I ONCE LOVED A BOY.

I once loved a boy, and a bold Irish boy,
    Far away in the hills of the West;
Ah! the love of that boy was my jewel of joy
    And I built him a bower in my breast,
        In my breast;
    And I built him a bower in my breast.

I once loved a boy, and I trusted him true,
    And I built him a bower in my breast;
But away, wirrasthrue! the rover he flew,
    And robbed my poor heart of its rest,
        Of its rest;
    And robbed my poor heart of its rest.

The spring-time returns, and the sweet speckled thrush
    Murmurs soft to his mate on her nest,
But forever there's fallen a sorrowful hush
    O'er the bower that I built in my breast,
        In my breast—
    O'er the desolate bower in my breast.

THE SONG OF THE FAIRY KING.

QUEEN of women, oh come away,
    Come to my kingdom strange to see ;
Where tresses flow with a golden glow,
    And white as snow is the fair body.

Under the arching of ebon brows
    Eyes of azure the soul enthral,
And a speech of songs to the mouth belongs,
    And sorrowful sighing shall ne'er befall.

Bright are the blooms of Innisfail,
    Green her forests wave in the west :
But brighter flowers and greener bowers
    Shall all be ours in that country blest.

Can her streams compare to the runnels rare
    Of yellow honey and rosy wine
That softly slip to the longing lip
    With magic flow through that land of mine?

We roam the earth in its grief and mirth,
   But move unseen of all therein,
For before their gaze there hangs a haze,
   The heavy haze of their mortal sin.

But our age wastes not, our beauty tastes not
   Evil's apple nor droops nor dies;
Death slays us never, but love for ever
   With stainless ardour illumes our eyes.

Then, queen of women, oh come away,
   Come and sit on my fairy throne,
In a realm of rest with spirits blest,
   Where sin and sorrow are all unknown.

WHEN SHE ANSWERED ME HER VOICE WAS LOW.

When she answered me her voice was low—but, oh!
    Not, Erin, thine own harp's impassioned chord
With prouder bliss e'er bade my bosom glow,
    Than she has kindled by that one sweet word.

When the colleen's eyes looked back the love in mine,
    My Erin, never after darkest night
With bluer welcome o'er the ocean line
    Thy shore has started on my patriot sight.

And, Erin, bid thy son as soon believe
    Thy song expired, thy star of promise set,
As dream my darling's eyes could e'er deceive,
    Her lips their low sweet answer all forget.

WITH FLUTTERING JOY.

How happy for the little birds
    From tree to tree, away and hither,
To pour their pretty, warbling words,
    And fly with fluttering joy together!
But let the sun rejoice the skies,
    Or sullen clouds his glory smother,
With heavy hearts we still must rise
    Far, far away from one another.

Now leave those foolish, feathered things,
    O Fortune, Fortune, fond and cruel!
And fit two pair of trusty wings
    Upon myself and Eileen jewel,
That she and I from earth may start,
    And skim the sky on angel feather,
Till from mid-heaven, heart to heart,
    With fluttering joy we fall together.

THE HOUR I PROVE FALSE.

The hour I prove false to my dark-headed darling,
    Let the grass grow to crimson, the frost fall in June;
The lark cease to sing, and the rook and the starling
    With the cuckoo and blackbird come changing their tune.

A long, long farewell, to my white-bosomed deary,
    And believe I'll be faithful whatever befall;
And of working to win you by day never weary,
    And by night never tire your dear face to recall.

Ah! branch of sweet bloom only cling on as faithful
    In that absence of years as you cling to me now,
For the hour you prove false Heaven and earth would grow hateful
    Since you called them to witness your young virgin vow.

'TIS A PITY I CAN'T SEE MY LOVE.

On his flute of gold the blackbird bold
Love's tale to his melting mate has told,
    And now the thieves have started;
And o'er the ground in fluttering round,
Enamoured fly, whilst you and I
    In lonesome pain are parted.
But when hearts beat true through the night of sorrow,
They're blest the more when the magic morrow
    Its rosy ray has darted.
Fortune may wave her wings and fly,
But she'll flutter back again by-and-by,
    And crown the constant-hearted.

These birds that pair in the April air
Forget their faith on the branches bare,
    By autumn blasts affrighted,
And to fresh loves sing with the start of spring;
When you and I with a golden ring
    In joy shall be united.

For when hearts beat true through the night of sorrow,
They're blest the most when the marriage morrow
    Its lamp of love has lighted.
    Fortune may wave her wings and fly,
    But she'll flutter back to us by-and-by,
    And crown the troth we've plighted.

SONG.

Life like ours is April weather;
    Tears and smiles, smiles and tears,
Sighs and laughter linked together;
    Fears and hopes, hopes and fears,
Storm and sunshine, hither, thither,
    Shifting through the spheres.

'Tis love alluring, harming, healing;
    Bliss his Yes! Woe his No!
Fortune's smile and frown revealing
    Foe in friend, friend in foe;
Mirth to-day, to-morrow Sorrow
    Guiding as we go.

GOOD-NIGHT.

Good-night! good-night! our feast is ended,
By young and old with smiles attended;
Where Wit and Worth and beauty blended,
   To speed the hours with dance and song.
      Beauty's smile
      Free from guile,
      Wit that shone
      Wounding none;
   And manly Worth and Woman true,
   Good-night! and joy go home with you!

Good-night! and may your minstrel's numbers
Still echo on amid your slumbers,
To spell-bind every care that cumbers
   The lover's heart, the mother's breast.
      Beauty, Mirth,
      Wit and Worth
      Fall to sleep,
      Calm and deep,
   Nor rouse, till rosy morrow call,
   "Awake, and joy go with you all!"

www.ingramcontent.com/pod-product-compliance
Lightning Source LLC
Chambersburg PA
CBHW020111170426
43199CB00009B/489